Exotic Car Facts

A PUNDIT'S GUIDE TO EXOTIC CARS

DEE ONEAL

ISBN: 978172407430
ISBN-13:

DEDICATION

"You may say I'm a dreamer, but I'm not the only one, I hope someday you'll join us, and the world will be as one"
-John Lennon

"Take the best that exists and make it better. If it doesn't exist, create it"
-Sir Henry Royce

"If you have to ask the price, you can't afford it "
-J.P. Morgan

"Imagine your dream, live it now"
-John Taylor Ewing

"Facts, not hacks"
-Dee Oneal

FOREWORD

"From Trailer Park to Aston Martin "
a Foreword by Neil Vitro

Cars captivated me in my youth, as they do so many others. My situation was a little different than most though. My parents were divorced when I was three, and I was raised by a single mother whose highest level of completed education was a high school diploma. This is in no way a sad story however, nor is it one that should be pitied. My mom was excellent. She worked hard and caved to the spoiled demands of her only child as often as possible. I never realized we were poor and besides, our 65 foot trailer was the biggest in the neighborhood...Fast forward to today, where I am a successful accountant and the proud owner of a Cobalt Blue Aston Martin Vantage. The friends I've made and professional network have been enhanced by being the owner of my dream exotic car. I wish that books like Exotic Car Facts had been available when I was younger because the opportunities that exist now to be part of this exotic car community are truly limitless. Thank you Dee for always telling it like it is, and as you always say "Facts, not hacks"

CONTENTS

ACKNOWLEDGMENTS

This book is dedicated to my family and friends for their tireless support and encouragement, and all of the people who have ever dreamed of owning an exotic car. If you can imagine your dream, it's time to live it **NOW**.

INTRODUCTION

Hello, and thank you for purchasing my book. If you're reading this book you've probably thought about the possibility of owning an exotic car, but didn't know the best way to go about getting one. If that's the case, I hope you will find this book helpful when considering to purchase your first exotic vehicle. Perhaps you already own an exotic car and are just curious about the title "A Pundit's Guide to Exotic Cars"; according to the English Oxford Dictionary, a pundit is "an expert in a particular subject or field who is frequently called upon to give his opinions to the public." So why am I talking about exotic cars? The reason is twofold:

One is that exotic cars are popular, desirable, visually engaging and eye catching. They are universally recognized as a symbol of prosperity, affluence and success and are often associated with visual representations of wealth. The second is because I've been in the automotive industry for years and as an exotic car owner and enthusiast I get asked all the time "what kind of work do you do to be able to drive an exotic car?" So I decided to share my experiences and strategies for how I have been able to own and drive exotic cars and turn them into a business venture that is profitable, scalable, and (most importantly) repeatable by just about anyone.

"If it's that easy, why isn't everyone doing it?" The truth is that many people are, (with varying degrees of success) but no one wants to share this secret with you. Why not? Because this revelation is so powerful and liberating, that it has the power to disrupt established industries. I'm here today because I want you to be able to create the lifestyle that you want, on your terms, to bring your dreams into focus and to encourage you to make them a reality. I want you to drive an exotic car too!

By no means is this book meant to be a comprehensive or exhaustive list of all of the various (or nefarious) ways to profit from exotic vehicles. It is an overview and recollection of purchasing exotic cars and my experiences with owning and profiting from them. Through the years I've had the opportunity to buy and drive some very nice cars. I've purchased brand new cars right off the showroom floor, certified pre-owned cars, used cars, leased cars, and have sold cars from almost every major brand, make and model. Even having prior experience, nothing compares to the excitement of buying your first real exotic vehicle.

This guide highlights popular and profitable exotic cars from what I consider to be the modern era, the 20 year time frame from 1999 through 2019. To me, 1999 represented a high point in the evolution, design and awareness of what a true "exotic car" is and 1999 was the year that the Ferrari 360 Modena went into production, which in my opinion is the quintessential embodiment of an exotic car. The Ferrari 360 set a new standard for the exotic car enthusiast. It was a relatively affordable and reliable supercar with outstanding performance, a timeless shape, and a sweeping design by Pininfarina that still endures to this day. The fact that this modern, mid-engine coupe by Ferrari is still coveted by admirers and enthusiasts exemplifies the definition of what a modern exotic sports car should be. The French describe it as "je ne sais quoi," the Italians call it "bellissimo," and in America we call it "bad-to-the-bone"; regardless of how you describe it, enthusiasm for exotic cars is universal.

1 DEFINITION OF AN EXOTIC CAR

SO JUST WHAT IS AN EXOTIC CAR?

Search for the word "exotic car" and you'll find a myriad of clichés and conjecture, originating from various sources regarding what precisely an exotic car is supposed to be. The opinions about what constitutes an exotic car are as varied as there are brands, makes, and models. Depending upon whom you ask, just about any rare, obscure or unusual car can be called "exotic", and they would be correct depending upon the specific context. Even though not everyone can agree about what an exotic car **"IS"** most people understand what it is **NOT**:

An exotic car is not cheap (but can become less expensive over time). Proprietary companies like Ferrari don't get the benefit of sharing technology and synergy that a vehicle produced by VW Group does, and so that also drives the cost of parts and development way up. Dealer maintenance can be costly, in many cases requiring proprietary parts and special tools or accessories. As a rule of thumb the more exotic the car is, the more expensive the repairs will be when something breaks.

An exotic car is not common (rarely seen in public). Exotic car owners consider themselves to be members of an exclusive club. The underlying impression is that if you can afford to drive an exotic car, chances are you have the means and ability to belong to the group. It's a comradery based on conspicuous consumption, and it works. Best friends and valuable business connections are made by virtue of driving the right car; it's like a secret social circle.

An exotic car is not reliable (search for "battery tender" in any exotic car forum). A BMW i8 might be considered "reliable" if you are comparing it to a Ferrari. And older exotic cars will typically have more issues than their newer brethren. However, depending on the brand, for example a Lamborghini Gallardo is more reliable than a Ferrari 360 Modena, which is extremely unreliable when compared to a modern Audi R8 V10 Plus. McLaren is in the same boat as Ferrari because it is in such a tight niche and suffers from minor but persistent development bugs.

An exotic car is not economical (you will never be accused of going "green" in an exotic) I'm reminded of a Facebook video I saw recently where a Prius driver tried to chastise a Lamborghini owner for exceeding the speed limit. Typically Exotic Cars require premium fuels, specialty fluids and consumable wear items such as brakes and tires made from exotic and rare materials that multiply the running costs exponentially. Not to mention that the average mpg of most exotic cars is an abysmal ten miles to the gallon, so trips to the filling station for petrol are frequent and often.

An exotic car is not practical (this is the only time you will see the words "practical" and "exotic car" in the same sentence). The trunk space is small and most exotic cars only have two real seats. This may not seem like a big deal but the first time you are out shopping and unable to fit all of your groceries, or want to carry more than one person, you will never forget how impractical and inconvenient your exotic car is.

CAN IT PASS THE "BADGE" TEST?

An exotic car should be easily recognized as being something unique or special, even in the absence of having a certain badge or brand. Would the car still be considered exceptional if it wasn't wearing a specific company logo? Can it stand on its own merits independent of any marketing and hype. Does the car sell itself? Is it unique in its design or based on an entry level model? Take off the badge and look at the car. If it no longer looks like an exotic car, then it's probably not. However, in order to narrow down the scope of this study and keep everything in a strict context, my definition of what makes an exotic car is based on the following four criteria:

Exclusively available

Low production volume

Bespoke and highly customized

Requires Proprietary Service.

EXCLUSIVELY AVAILABLE.

When it comes to the world of motor vehicles, nothing captures the imagination of an automotive enthusiast quite like an exotic car. Many people confuse exotic cars with high performing sports cars and luxury vehicles such as offerings available from Porsche, Audi, BMW, Jaguar, Mercedes Benz, Lexus, Infiniti and Acura to name a few, but the truth is that there are fewer truly exotic cars around than people imagine. Brands like Ferrari,

Lamborghini, Aston Martin, Bentley, Rolls Royce, Koenigsegg, McLaren, Pagani as well as the handful of boutique coach-builders who only produce exceptional vehicles of rare quality, without compromise. They are equally loved by dreamers, drivers and car collectors alike who are willing to pay the premium these vehicles command. When purchased new, these vehicles can be prohibitively expensive, and many times they sell at a premium well above MSRP. Exotic cars have massive appeal because of what they represent: Exclusivity.

An exotic car is the ultimate status symbol, owned by few to the envy of many. However, if a vehicle is mass produced, has several iterations over the years and there are thousands of examples available on the roads, then it's definitely not an exotic car.

LOW PRODUCTION VOLUME.

There are only a handful of manufacturers that consistently produce models that fit into this narrow criteria. Some of the most well known: Aston Martin, Bugatti, Koenigsegg, Ferrari, Lamborghini, McLaren, Pagani. Notably absent from this list are some well known marques such as Audi, Bentley, BMW, Mercedes Benz, Porsche, Rolls Royce and others. The reason being even though they have produced and/or do offer exotic cars as halo vehicles for their respective brands, that is not their core focus, as more pedestrian offerings such as sports coupes, luxury vehicles, suvs, and sedans also wear their moniker and as such cannot be considered. Examples of exotic cars offered by those brands (and others) will be mentioned later on in a chapter dedicated to specific makes and models.

Exotic cars are produced in extremely limited numbers, and because of the high degree of engineering and technology, they are used for professionally sanctioned racing events. Many manufacturers use this high visibility to market and promote their brand to potential buyers of their vehicles in other segments of the vehicle market. Based on annual production numbers since 1999, there are probably fewer than 250,000 or so true "exotic cars" available worldwide. Think about that for a moment: only 250,000 exotic cars available to satisfy global demand. Talk about scarcity. For example, when considering the Ferrari 360 Modena which was produced from 1999 through 2005, there were only approximately 17,000 produced in total (including variants such as the Spyder and Stradale). The Bugatti Veyron is even more rare, with fewer than 500 total examples produced since its introduction in 2005. The most prolific Lamborghini model ever made was the Gallardo, with only around 14,000 total units produced in its 10 year time span beginning in 2003. McLaren to date has produced less than 15,000 cars, total. Koenigsegg, less than 125 in all. Pagani has an ambitious target of producing 50 cars per year. Even at maximum capacity since its origin in 1999, there would only be 1000 produced to date. Aston Martin has one of the longest histories, over 100 years, and has produced less than 50,000 vehicles total.

BESPOKE AND HIGHLY CUSTOMIZED.

An exotic car fits into several categories: limited production, superior engineering, high performance, incorporate rare materials, progressive styling, aggressively designed, hand made, prohibitively expensive, and highly desirable. These vehicles are enhanced in performance and radical in appearance. Exotic cars are characterized by high quality, comfort, innovative design, technologically advanced, ultra modern, and incorporate features which project an image of status. Exotic cars are also found in the super-niche, ultra premium, ultra luxury, high performance segment of the automotive world. Because of this an exotic car is defined as a niche, high performance, premium, luxury or ultra luxury sports car. By virtue of their very nature and what they represent exotic cars are literally a "one-off" creation.

Exotic cars are often built by hand and created from unique or advanced materials such as high-grade leather, alcantara, Kevlar, aluminum, titanium and carbon fiber, as well as incorporating rare elements like halogen, nitrogen, gold, silver, diamonds and other precious gems and jewels. Because of their limited availability and the investment of time and resources that goes into making an exotic car, the fortunate few who are able to acquire them first-hand get to pick and choose and help guide the final look and design of the finished work of art. The exotic car is the canvas and the lucky owner is the artist, carefully picking and choosing and selecting the color palette, materials and options they want incorporated into the design of the exotic car. Lamborghini offers what it calls its "Ad Personam" customization program where buyers of a new Lamborghini get to pick and choose their options, Ferrari offers a personalization program called "One-to-One" that lets you build your own Ferrari. Custom coach-builder Pagani dedicated a model to his late friend and created the Huayra BC, and McLaren Special Operations (MSO) says that they create exotic cars around the owner's tastes and preferences offering a truly bespoke, ultra-exclusive experience.

REQUIRES PROPRIETARY SERVICE

Finding a competent technician to service an exotic car can sometimes be more difficult than finding a needle-in-a-haystack. And locating an authorized mechanic is just the beginning, the other consideration is cost. At some point your exotic car will require service, be it new tires, brakes, an oil change or any other maintenance required in the course of owning the vehicle. Considering that an exotic car is the equivalent of driving a race car on a public street, the maintenance cost is comparable to what you would expect if you were campaigning a race car on a racetrack. McLaren is especially notorious in this regard with annual service costs over a thousand dollars, Ferrari maintenance is equally costly, a few hundred for an oil change, and major services potentially costing five-figures. Bugatti's schedule service is legendary: $20,000 for an oil change, annual service is $30,000 and a new set of wheels and tires totaling more than the price of a decent starter home at over $120,000. Lamborghini often requires that the engine be taken out for service.

If you need major service on your Koenigsegg or Pagani you might be looking at shipping your vehicle back to its country of origin for support. The reason for such extreme costs associated with keeping an exotic vehicle running is that in many cases, a portion of the vehicle will need to be disassembled and removed just to gain access to the engine for service, which necessitates that the vehicle is essentially being "rebuilt" every time it needs maintenance. Exotic cars aren't built to be practical, they're built to be fast, beautiful, and extreme, ergo, the cost to keep these vehicles in peak shape and tip-top performance is equally extreme. So, now that we understand what an exotic car is, let's take a look at the reason why they cost so much in the first place.

2 WHY EXOTIC CARS ARE EXPENSIVE

There are several reasons why exotic cars are so expensive:

SCARCITY.

It's simple economics, supply (or lack thereof) and demand. There just aren't that many exotic cars made, and of the ones that are produced, losses due to various means of attrition further deplete the number of exotic cars available. Over a long enough timeline, fewer and fewer high-quality examples remain, and this adds to their appeal, and price, as collectors and enthusiasts alike covet these rare vehicles.

The Fallacy of Supply and Demand. People purchase exotic cars based on perceived value, quality or availability and often on all three. The methods of appointing a value to an object with no previous value, like a Bugatti Chiron, is susceptible to irrational pricing. When consumers buy a product at a certain price, they become "anchored" to that price, (i.e. they associate the initial price with the same product over a period of time.) An anchor price of a certain object, say a new exotic car, will affect the way they perceive the value of all exotic cars under consideration. Other prices will seem low or high in relation to the original anchor. And every year the cost of the latest exotic car increases in a seeming race to see which brand can be the most expensive. At the time of this writing, the new Bugatti Divo has just been announced with an estimated price tag of $5.8 Million dollars (USD).

BUILD QUALITY.

Another reason why exotic cars seem so expensive is due to the amount of time and labor that goes into creating them – people are willing to wait for quality, that's a fact. Exotic cars are no exception. Consider this: it takes over 20 hours to make a single Hermes Birkin bag. If you aren't familiar with them, they are some of the most exclusive (and expensive) handbags ever made. The basic rules of economics apply, the more rare an item is, the more difficult it is to make or acquire, the more desirable it becomes. So, to put this into the context of an exotic car, I have created a hypothetical example of what the estimated material costs, labor etc. of building an exotic car could be (e.g. how many meters or kg of carbon fiber were used during construction, price per meter/kg, etc.)

MATERIALS COST (BASED ON CARBON FIBER WEIGHT): 0.3 LBS / SQFT, COST: $1.67 (RAW CLOTH) - $20 (FINISHED)/SQFT. AVERAGE WEIGHT OF AN EXOTIC CAR IS AROUND 3,000 LBS, 3,000 LBS ÷ 0.3 LBS/SQFT =10,000 SQFT. 10,000 SQFT × $20.00/SQFT = $200,000 IN JUST CARBON FIBER WORK.

LABOR: IT CAN TAKE ANYWHERE FROM 24 TO 48 HOURS TO COMPLETE ASSEMBLY OF THE AVERAGE EXOTIC CAR, ONCE ALL OF THE PIECES ARE CREATED. IT WOULD TAKE JUST OVER TWO DAYS TO COMPLETELY ASSEMBLE AN AVENTADOR, IF IT WERE LAID OUT LIKE A JIGSAW PUZZLE, BUT THE REALITY IS THAT CREATING AN EXOTIC CAR BY HAND IS MUCH MORE COMPLICATED THAN THAT. IN ITALY, AUTO MANUFACTURING FACTORY WORKERS EARN $46,700 (£37,600) ANNUALLY; THE AVERAGE SALARY IS 21.30 EUROS (£18.15) PER HOUR. $22/HR × 18 HOURS = $396 (LABOR COST TO MAKE A LAMBORGHINI), $393,695 ÷ $396 = 994 (ROUGHLY 1000 TIMES THE COST OF LABOR). BY COMPARISON, IN ORDER TO PRODUCE THE AUDI R8, 70 EMPLOYEES ASSEMBLE OVER 5,000 PARTS BY HAND AND CAN PRODUCE A MAXIMUM OF 30 UNITS DAILY. THE ENGINE, DRIVELINE, TRANSMISSION AND OTHER VARIOUS COMPONENTS OF A LAMBORGHINI COST ROUGHLY $50,000 TO ASSEMBLE AND INSTALL. (HEAVEN ONLY KNOWS HOW MUCH ENGINEERING EFFORT WAS INVESTED IN DEVELOPING THE ENGINE AND OTHER CRITICAL COMPONENTS.)

Thus from this very basic example the estimated production costs to build a supercar such as the Aventador are relatively high. In the United States, the cost of an Aventador retails at $393,695 Msrp. The car likely costs upwards of $250,000 or more to manufacture.

INTRINSIC VALUE.

The fact is an exotic car is not a mode of transportation (although it is functionally designed as such), it's a work of art. The overwhelming cost of production and acquisition is more akin to a real estate purchase than to a consumer appliance intended to be disposable; consumed by depreciation until it essentially becomes worthless. Due to this misconception, many people abuse their exotic car through excessive usage and ultimately suffer great financial losses due to subscribing to the belief that an exotic car should be used in the same way that a common passenger vehicle is utilized, for daily and frequent driving and transportation. It's like painting over a Picasso, or using the statue of David as a lawn ornament. Capital assets like real estate, yachts, private aircraft, luxury items, and exotic cars especially, with a high initial retail value, will rarely depreciate to zero ($0), if well maintained and with limited use because of their retained intrinsic value. In most case, even after an extended period of time, they still can easily retain at least 50% or more of their initial retail value if treated as an investment. Fun fact: It's estimated that 65% of all Rolls-Royce automobiles ever made are still on the road today. Same thing with Porsche: Over 70% of all Porsche vehicles ever built are still on the road today. True quality never dies.

3 EXOTIC CAR MARKET OVERVIEW

MAKES, MODELS, AND BRANDS.

Taking a look at the automotive industry, there is not a market segment designated as "exotic car". In fact, the vehicle segment that most closely correlates to most people's idea of an exotic car is called the "luxury or super luxury" segment, which also encompasses/includes sedans, crossovers, and suvs. On the basis of body type, it includes 2 Door, 4 Door and SUV. The global luxury car market has increased significantly during the years 2010-2017 and projections are made that the market will continue to rise in the next four years tremendously (i.e. 2018-2022). Based on my criteria, the list of vehicles that are considered strictly "exotic cars" is relatively short; so don't be offended if your favorite vehicle didn't make the list. For example, the BMW M3 is a great high performance luxury sedan, but due to its high production volume and wide accessibility, it just isn't and exotic car. Same thing applies to the base model Porsche 911, not exotic, not rare, uber cool and definitely a high performance luxury sports car, but just not an exotic car. Audi makes some great cars as well, but the majority of them are not exotic cars. The key players in the global luxury car market segment are BMW, Daimler AG, Volkswagen and Ferrari, who are also profiled with their financial information and respective business strategies. In the United States where I live, only four premium makes (Mercedes-Benz, BMW, Acura and Audi) offer competitive products in their respective core categories. Luxury premium car makers offer competitive entries in the luxury vehicle segment, but they are usually not exotic cars but instead are classified as "Sporty Luxury Cars" also known as "Sports and Sporty Cars." So the closest match by definition to a true exotic car, is what is classified as the Premium Sports Car market segment. And what cars do we find on this list? The Acura NSX, Audi R8, BMW i8, Dodge Viper, Ford GT, Lexus LFA, Mercedes Amg GT, Nissan GTR and Porsche 911. By now I'm sure that you are wondering what exotic cars made the cut, so without further ado, here is my list of the most popular exotic cars of the modern era.

4 MY FAVORITE EXOTIC CARS OF THE MODERN ERA

ASTON MARTIN

Aston Martin is a British exotic car maker with a very long and storied history. Founded in 1913, AM is widely recognized as one of the most expensive and luxurious exotic cars in the world. Known affectionately as the "James Bond" exotic car brand, Aston Martin is considered a British cultural icon. Beginning in 2001, AM released the V12 Vanquish and Vanquish S, 2004 Aston Martin DB9, 2005 AM V8 and 12 Vantage, 2007 AM DBS V12, 2009 AM One-77, 2010 AM Rapide and Rapide S, 2012 Virage and Volante, and 2016 AM DB11. To date, only the Vantage and DB11 are still in production.

What makes this exotic car special: Aston Martin is one of the last of a dying breed: manual transmission, V12 engines, low production volumes, bespoke British design and styling. Aston Martin evokes images of a Gentleman's sports car as this Grand Tourer has massive road presence. There is something unmistakable about seeing the proud visage of an Aston Martin on the open road. The sheer versatility of this brand makes any Aston

Martin on this list a great addition to one's exotic car collection.

AUDI (R8)

Introduced in 2006 by Audi AG in Germany, the Audi R8 is considered by many as the quintessential every man's exotic car combining the best aspects of the exotic car experience in measured doses that just about anyone can appreciate. Based on the Lamborghini Gallardo, the R8 incorporated a revolutionary aluminum space frame design, with judicious use of carbon fiber, particularly in their signature CF side blades. The first generation ran from 2006 through 2015; (2012 if you are considering only the 4.2L FSI) with and estimated total of only 29,000 units produced globally. 2009 saw the introduction of the 5.2L FSI which utilized the 5.2L V10 from the Gallardo. In 2010, Audi introduced a Spyder variant and a limited production R8 GT version. Taking a brief hiatus in 2013, Audi reintroduced the second generation R8, touting more horsepower, redesigned looks and a 7-speed S-tronic dual clutch.

What makes this exotic car special: The Audi R8 is a mid-engine, all-wheel-drive Quattro, and those iconic carbon-fiber side blades make the Audi R8 unique. The Audi R8 seamlessly blends fluid Italian-inspired styling with German precision and performance. It's difficult to find a bad angle on an Audi R8, and the design aesthetic combines equal parts minimalism and extravagance with a dash of drama added in for good measure. Once you've owned an Audi R8, you will always want one in your stable.

BENTLEY (CONTINENTAL GT)

Bentley, under the auspices of it's parent company Volkswagen AG, released the first iteration of the Bentley Continental GT in 2003. British in design and utilizing German mass production manufacturing methods, Bentley is one of the most prolific and popular luxury exotic cars in the world. In 2005 Bentley released an updated version of the GT with their Mulliner Specification, 2006 saw the GTC convertible and again in 2007 with the Diamond series, limited to a reported 400 units worldwide. 2008 introduced the GT Speed and in 2009 the limited production Supersports. The second generation came in 2011, and most notable was the 2014 update that introduced the GT3-R limited to only 300 units. The 3rd and current generation was announced for 2018.

What makes this exotic car special: The Bentley Continental GT combines the best of both worlds: British style and sensibilities combined with German precision. The 6.0L W12 twin-turbo engines and 8-speed transmissions are the pinnacle of automotive performance. The road presence of the Bentley is the reason it is one of the most purchased exotic cars in the world today.

BMW (I8)

In 2014 German luxury automaker BMW introduced a hybrid sports car called the i8. This hybrid turbo-charged vehicle is striking in design and its limited production makes it a desirable exotic car. As of 2016, more than 10,000 BMW i8's have been produced; In 2018 the i8 roadster variant was introduced.

What makes this exotic car special: The i8 is an innovative step forward in the world of exotics. With its pleasing visual aesthetic and hybrid electric technology, the i8 is the world's best-selling electric hybrid sports car. The biggest common criticism surrounding the i8 is BMW's use of amplified engine sounds (i.e. the fake engine noises), which is closely followed up by the lack of power. Which is a relative thing, because compared to the average automobile the BMW is very quick and any shortcomings are quickly overlooked when you open those signature vertical doors.

BUGATTI

Once again the Volkswagen Automobile Group in association with one of its subsidiaries Bugatti, produced a mid-engined super sports exotic car which they dubbed the Veyron. Introduced in 2005 as the Veyron, 2009 as the Grand Sport, 2010 the Super Sport, and 2012 the Grand Sport Vitesse, the Bugatti and all its variants were widely recognized as the most expensive and fastest, street-legal production exotic cars in the world. In the past 10 years, only an estimated 450 total Bugatti Veyrons (including all sub-variants) were produced worldwide, with production officially ending in 2015 to make way for its successor the Bugatti Chiron.

What makes this exotic car special: The 8.0L quad-turbocharged W16 engine makes the Bugatti a legitimate 1000 horsepower exotic car that is street-legal and can be reliably driven daily without incident, or so they say. There will always be faster cars with more horsepower but no production vehicle can boast the same level of detail that a Bugatti does; it's literally an objet d'art on wheels.

FERRARI

Possibly the best known, and most recognizable exotic car brand in the world, Ferrari made a quantum leap forward in the year 2000 with the introduction of the Ferrari 360 Modena. The 360, with its space-frame aluminum chassis and signature styling provided by Pininfarina, was a formal introduction to many people, by Ferrari, to the world of exotic cars. This low-volume exotic car is still widely recognized today and appreciated by aficionados and the casual observer alike. Less than 20,000 total units were produced in the five-year period between 1999 and 2005 including the three variants: Modena, Spider and Challenge Stradale. In 2004 Ferrari produced the sequel to it's successful 360 with the F430 which was an improvement on the 360 line. In 2005, the F430 Spider joined the line up. 2009 saw the release of Ferrari's next Pininfarina-inspired project; an entirely new model designed from the ground up called the Ferrari 458, and subsequently continues through to the Ferrari 488, released in 2015 through the present day.

What makes this exotic car special: The Ferrari 360 was the benchmark for the modern exotic car era. Arguably the first relatively reliable exotic car of the modern era. With its authentic Italian design, many would agree that Ferrari is the definitive exotic car brand in the world. Owning a Ferrari is a love-hate relationship; few exotic cars are equally inspiring and infuriating (usually expressing those traits at the same time). It takes a special kind of exotic car enthusiast to own a Ferrari and indulge in all of it's subtle nuances and quirks, but if you can live with them, the Ferrari is the king of high-maintenance exotic cars.

FORD (GT)

In 2005, American car company Ford released it's 5.4L Supercharged V8 dubbed the Ford GT. An homage to the original Ford GT40 race car, only around 4,000 Ford GTs were made for their first generation run ending quickly in 2006. Almost a decade later in 2016, Ford reintroduced the GT in another limited production run, projecting to only produce 250 per year, at an estimated rate of about one car per day.

What makes this exotic car special: One of the few truly exotic cars made in America, the Ford GT demonstrated to the world that domestic auto manufacturers have the ability, if not always the motivation or audience, to design and build a world-class exotic car. Until challenged by the latest iterations of the Corvette ZR1, and Dodge Viper ACR, there were no major manufactured American supercars that could rival the design and performance of the original Ford GT. God Bless America!

LAMBORGHINI

The years 2003-2013 marked a turning point in design for Italian car maker Lamborghini who introduced their best selling and most prolific model ever, the Gallardo. With just over 14,000 units produced, the Gallardo firmly cemented Lamborghini as the exotic car of choice for the masses, and made way for its successor the Lamborghini Huracan. The V10 powered Gallardo, and it's Audi counterpart, the Audi R8, ushered in a new era of comparatively affordable and reliable exotic cars. With F1-inspired technology, such as the infamous "E-gear" single clutch manumatic transmission and 520 horsepower, the Gallardo is one of the most famous and enduring, as well as highly sought after exotic cars of this era.

What makes this exotic car special: The Lamborghini Gallardo is one of the most collectible exotic cars on the planet. The raging bull insignia is an unmistakable Lamborghini trademark, and owning one grants you admission to a unique fraternity. Overall, the fit and finish is lacking, but the visceral driving experience and adrenaline rush when you are in the cockpit of this jet-fighter on wheels is the salve that helps you forget some of its shortcomings. Every serious exotic car collector or enthusiast should get some seat-time in a Lamborghini, at least once in their life.

To round out my list, I will briefly highlight the top ten brands in the realm of luxury vehicles and exotic cars: Aston Martin, Bentley, Bugatti,

Ferrari, Koenigsegg, Lamborghini, Mercedes, Pagani, Porsche and Rolls-Royce. Although the order of appearance often changes, these ten exotic car manufacturers are often listed among the best of the best in the world of luxury vehicles. The most costly exotic cars on the planet are aren't just about transportation; these moving objets d'art epitomize the ideals of the "one percent" and in that universe, flashiness and swagger outweigh logic and frugality. Luxury lifestyles aside, these mind-boggling machines are engineering marvels, and who wouldn't relish the opportunity to get behind the wheel of something so ludicrously impractical that it somehow just makes sense?

To reiterate, this is just a list of the exotic cars that I feel represent the mainstays of the modern exotic car world. There are many other vehicles that are worthy of consideration: the Lotus Evora and Exige, Nissan GTR, Acura NSX, Porsche 911 Turbo and GT series cars, BMW M-series, Maserati, Mercedes AMGs, and the list goes on…and a reasonable argument could be made for their inclusion on anyone's list of desirable and collectible exotic cars, but in an effort to narrow down the field and distill the concept to its purest essence, I focused on exotic cars that I believe are indisputable. So now that we know what an exotic car is and why they cost so much, the question you may be asking yourself is "who is buying these exotic cars…and why?"

5 PERKS AND PERILS OF OWNERSHIP

PROFILE OF AN EXOTIC CAR OWNER

Statistically men are more likely to be exotic car owners as scientists have discovered a correlation between increased testosterone and ownership of high-status luxury items, like exotic cars. According to one university study, men who drive exotic cars are considered to be more attractive by women; the implication being that some women are attracted to wealth and status. Also, scientists found that a single dose of testosterone was enough to boost men's preference for higher status goods.

In another popular study, scientists noted a marked increase in the testosterone levels of test subjects who drove a Porsche vs a Toyota Camry. In actual practice I don't know of too many women that are solely impressed by an exotic car. I have noticed an inordinate amount of attention received from other males. Be prepare to spend and extra 10-15 minutes at the gas station as random people will want to ask you questions about yourself and your exotic car. Most of the questions are innocuous and after answering the question several times, you will have memorized an appropriate response to the usual queries.

The amount of attention you receive in public places is a very good indication of whether your vehicle is an exotic car or not. From the moment you start driving an exotic car, you will begin to notice that people will start following your vehicle and watching you. Their interest will be piqued and assumptions about your wealth will be made. Just like wearing a nice suit to a business meeting, an exotic car is an attention getter that makes a strong statement about you and will be a topic curiosity and of conversation.

PERCEPTION VS REALITY OF EXOTIC CAR OWNERSHIP

Theories related to consumer buying habits suggest that the decision to buy an exotic car is to impress, and could be motivated by a desire to improve social standing, compensate for personal or emotional reasons, or a combination of all of the above. Regardless, exotic cars are status markers of invidious distinction, inspiring envy in others through overt displays of wealth and power, intentionally or intentionally, consciously or subconsciously. In my opinion people have different motives for purchasing exotic cars, some relate to a desire for quality, others relish the exclusivity of owning something rare, some want to demonstrate that they can afford an exotic car, some for self-affirmation, some for self-validation. Status seeking is a prevalent source of motivation, especially in today's social media society. Look no further than Instagram and you will discover millions of profiles displaying images of lavish living and the luxury lifestyle. Whatever your reasons may be, ultimately people who seek to own an exotic car are car enthusiasts at heart and have an appreciation for exotic cars and car culture. Now that you know and understand what an exotic car really is and why you should buy one, you may be asking yourself "How can I afford it?" and "When do I start making some money?" Those answers are found in the next section.

6 PREPARING FOR YOUR 1ST EXOTIC CAR

HOW MUCH DOES IT COST TO OWN AN EXOTIC CAR?

One of the most popular questions on the internet is "how much does it cost to own an exotic car?" Contrary to popular belief the answer is very simple and straightforward. There are numerous online payment calculators that can estimate fairly accurately what your payment for a given car loan would be, credit score withstanding. So what people are really wondering is "how does that guy afford to own an exotic car?" and furthermore "how can I be **THAT** guy with the exotic car?"

Upon closer inspection there are a few different scenarios that can explain the where, why, and who of exotic car ownership:

People are leasing new exotic cars. Leasing an exotic car is by far the easiest and most convenient way to get behind the wheel of a brand new factory fresh exotic car. The credit criteria and financial qualifications to lease an exotic car are almost identical to what it takes to purchase one outright. If you own a business that allows you to justify the lease on your exotic car as a deductible expense then you are ahead of the game. Good for you.

People are renting exotic cars. Exotic car rental is common in major metropolitan areas and for those people who are not ashamed to "fake it until they make it" renting an exotic car is just as good as owning it, at least until it's time to turn it back in.

People are ridiculously wealthy and buy whatever they want. Never discount the fact that there are many high net worth individuals in the world that can afford to buy new cars like most people buy shoes. It happens all day, every day. If you don't know a high net worth individual, then it's time to expand your social circle. You're probably living next door to a millionaire, and just don't know it…yet.

People are financing used and pre-owned exotic cars. Used or pre-owned exotic cars are one of the main ways that people are able to afford to purchase exotic cars. Exotic cars change slowly and many models make almost imperceptible changes during their entire production run. So to the untrained eye or the uninformed an older vehicle, in good condition will most likely look as good as a newer model. And due to their rarity and scarcity the chance of someone seeing any exotic car, let alone a brand new one is very slim. So everything looks new, the first time you see it. So for example, a $100,000 car loan financed for 72 months with 20% down and decent credit would put your payment somewhere around $1500/month roughly. If you have $20k to put down, can secure financing, and the ability to devote about $2k per month to exotic car payments, then yes you too can own an exotic car

The next most frequently asked question is "what kind of exotic car should I buy?" to which I answer in kind with a question of my own which is: why are you wanting to buy an exotic car? Or more specifically what kind of buyer are you: a Collector-Connoisseur or a Driver-Enthusiast? What is the right exotic car for you?

7 TWO DIFFERENT TYPES OF BUYERS

TWO DIFFERENT TYPES OF BUYERS

Why make this distinction you may ask? Because the type of consumer you are and your intended purpose/reason for wanting an exotic car (and how you intend to use it) will greatly influence the price you pay upfront, as well as what the ongoing cost of ownership will be. The residual value of the car is what it's worth when you decide to sell it, either for a net profit or a loss. By planning ahead and utilizing the proper strategy, you can mitigate your losses and increase the enjoyment of your exotic car during your time of ownership.

The Driver (Enthusiast). For the person who wants to not only be seen but also experience the exotic car as it was intended to be used. Driver-quality cars are either used as a weekend ride or recreationally, although in some cases it can also be used for daily transportation. Due to the rarity, and high performance nature, and poor fuel economy, daily-driving an exotic car is not generally recommended. But there are still those brave souls who are willing to sacrifice a little (or a lot of) comfort for performance and are willing to take the risk. Purchasing an exotic car that is intended to be driven frequently has some benefits. The criteria for a driver's quality car is less focused on the pedigree and condition of the vehicle and more towards the mechanical condition and overall superficial appearance. A vehicle with slight cosmetic imperfections or minor body damage that does not impact a critical area like the engine, suspension, chassis or frame and that has been properly repaired by a competent body/repair shop should not be immediately dismissed from consideration, and in fact should be the better choice for a vehicle that is intended to be driven and enjoyed often in its natural habitat.

The Collector (Connoisseur). A collector-quality exotic car is typically one with exceptionally low mileage, somewhere below 5k, and in some rare cases 10k max. This car will be in excellent condition with very minimal visible wear and usage. A clean Carfax and complete service records and proper chain of custody/clean title. Multiple owners are not uncommon although an academic argument in favor of fewer owners can be made. To the Collector/Connoisseur, a high quality exotic car is typically regarded as an investment and as such they can expect to pay a premium for an excellent example; the goal being to buy-and-hold the car for a longer period of time until the market is attractive enough to sell it for a profit. These cars are not typically driven often if at all, as rare cars of this caliber are highly sensitive to mileage-based depreciation. The ancillary costs associated with curating, storing and archiving an exotic car collection can often mount quickly and unless you have the ability to buy and hold for a very long time, but there are few other asset-classes to collect that are as exciting as a rare collection of exotic vehicles.

When deciding to buy a collector-qulity exotic car a few questions to consider are: How long do you anticipate keeping the exotic car before you sell it? Where will you store it/garage it? How ofter will you drive it? Will you be able to maintain the current condition of the car? Will you have adequet insurance coverage in the event of a total loss? All very important questions to consider as a collector looking to reap a net profit from ownership of a collector-quality exotic car; most people only consider the acquisition cost and the exit value, but the actual net result is the big picture to consider. My personal opinion regarding collecting exotic cars can be summed up by a story from my youth. As a kid, I was passionate about comic books. I loved the artwork, the stories were entertaining, and they helped stimulate my imagination while simultaneously instilling a desire for reading, and I became an avid reader. As I grew older, I became aware of the potential for collecting comic books as a hobby, for profit, which stressed acquiring the most popular issues and keeping them in pristine condition. So, while my collection of comic books increased, my overall enjoyment decreased, because I rarely actually read the stories anymore. I was just focused on hunting down and collecting the most financially lucrative titles and cultivating my collection, in the hopes of holding them long enough to reap a handsome profit. Through a series of unfortunate events, I lost over half of the thousands of comic books I had collected over the years. My biggest regret was that I hadn't even gotten the satisfaction of reading most of them, not even once.

8 SALVAGED AND STORIED EXOTIC CARS

AN OBSERVATION ON SALVAGED EXOTIC CARS.

If the goal is to actually drive your exotic car, frequently and with enthusiasm, then the objective should be to target a vehicle that is mechanically sound and in excellent running condition, with less emphasis placed on factors like the number of owners, "high" mileage (for an exotic), cosmetic blemishes or minor aesthetic flaws and superficial accident or collision damage that does not impact critical components of the vehicle, such as the frame, engine, drivetrain, electronics or suspension. In this regard, exotic cars with salvage titles and branded titles (lemons or buybacks) can often present a tantalizing opportunity to daily-drive an exotic car, while minimizing the risks associated with ownership. Consider this: if you've ever followed any racing series, such as LeMans, or the 24 Hour race at Daytona, you've likely seen many of the same exotic cars that you have dreamed of racing (and often crashing), sustaining significant damage and abuse. That's what they were designed to do, and they execute this surprisingly well. While walking through the garage paddock at one such race, I asked the technicians what would happen to the wrecked Gallardo they just pulled off the track. Their answer was curt: "we will repair it and have it back in the race within the hour". If a high performance racing team can repair critical body and frame damage on an exotic car and trust that it will perform on a racetrack at sustained high speeds, then I believe a daily-driven exotic car can manage with a little bumper rash, curbed wheels and a few dents and dings without being a cause of major concern.   The only time cosmetic damage should be a concern is if you are a serious car collector and your purpose is to curate a collection of exotic cars that will be shown but not driven, or you are speculating on the market and hoping to maximize your profit when you sell.   Unless you are a collector, there is absolutely no reason to pay a premium for a collection-grade exotic car, especially if your intention is to daily-drive an exotic car.   There are just too many uncontrolled variables on public roads and highways to risk exposing a collector quality exotic car to the road.   So save yourself some anxiety and some money and buy the right exotic car for the intended purpose that you want to use it for.

UNDERSTANDING DEPRECIATION TO MITIGATE RISK.

Purchasing any vehicle for the purpose of using it as transportation is a liability.   The risks associated with utilizing an exotic car as transportation compounds these risks exponentially.   Everything associated with ownership of an exotic car is multiplied by a factor of "X";   insurance, storage, maintenance, and consumables such as fuel, brakes, body repair and tires are all more expensive when you own an exotic car.   The one saving grace that helps offset the tremendous expense and liability of owning a depreciating "asset" such as an exotic car is the fact that certain exotic cars stop depreciating as rapidly after a few years.   There tends to be a limit to how far a well-optioned exotic car will fall.   After all, when was the last time you saw a Lamborghini, Ferrari, or Bugatti in the bargain bullpen of a used car lot?   Active depreciation due to frequent use, excessive mileage, accident/collision damage or wear and tear will ruin an exotic car's value significantly.   An average of two to three thousand miles per year is acceptable. Anticipating model changes is critical as a significant update or even a new model comes out every eight to ten years. You can see why, when selecting an exotic car, it is important to decide early on whether you are going to be a Driver or Collector. Now that you've decided what kind of exotic car owner you are, the next step is to figure out which exotic car you want!

9 TRUTH ABOUT MMR & AUCTIONS

THE TRUTH ABOUT DEALER WHOLESALE AND PUBLIC AUCTIONS.

Whether you are talking about Manheim Dealer auctions (The Manheim Market Report or MMR, is an indictor of wholesale prices in the automotive trade) or Ebay Auto listings the truth is that they are all both just another form of wholesale. The open market auction format is no different than what dealers do every day at the "dealer only" auctions. Manheim Market Reports are popular among dealers, brokers, and buyers, because it is a reasonably accurate snapshot of trading activity of a target market. Keep in mind however that a majority of the highest quality exotic cars are not sold at auction and never advertised in a public forum. Private party sales of high quality exotic cars is the norm. Most boutique exotic car dealerships operate on consignment to help their clients more in and out of their exotic cars. With few exceptions, a majority of vehicles that you see offered at dealer-only auctions will have some flaw that will need to be addressed in the reconditioning process. Dealer auctions are a great place for enthusiasts to find a dependable exotic car intended to be driven daily without regard to mileage or conservation of a pristine condition. Keep in mind that at the end of the day, it is the open market that determines what an exotic car is worth (i.e. It's only worth what someone is willing to write a check for.)

The laws of supply and demand apply, especially in the case of exotic cars due to their high degree of intrinsic value, and at the end of the day, the goal of any profitable car dealership is to make the most money. The definition of wholesale is: The cost of a good sold by a wholesaler (i.e. a market price). The wholesaler will usually charge a price somewhat higher than he or she paid, and the retailer who purchases the goods from the wholesaler will increase the price again when they sell. So, in order to get a good feel for what an exotic car is selling for, and what your target acquisition price should be, check the completed listings on open marketplaces like EBay, James Edition, Facebook, and also the various forums to see what people are actually paying for a particular make and model of exotic vehicle that you are interested in.

Compare apples to apples and look for comparable features and options, but realize at the end of the day the vehicle's mileage and overall condition are the two biggest factors in determining its value. A majority of exotic car owners will typically trade in their vehicle through a dealership, as it is one of the fastest and most efficient ways to dispose of your old car and also secure a newer vehicle. That being said, the dealer will always offer you much less than you could get from selling the car privately, but when you weigh the cost of saving time and aggravation in dealing with potential buyers, it's often worth it in the end. It's better to dance with the devil that you know, and in most cases a dealership will want to protect their reputation and stimulate repeat business, so it behooves them to act professionally and accordingly. If you are determined to sell your exotic car privately, consider what the cost to replace the vehicle would be. Could you buy your current car, for less than what you are trying to sell it for? If the answer is no, then you are in the right vehicle; always buy low and sell high in order to maintain a healthy profit margin. Replace your exotic car only when you can purchase at actual cash value, or sell for a profit.

You make your money when you initially purchase your exotic car, not when you get ready to sell it. Forecast how long you want to keep the car and then plan how you will get out of it; if you don't know what the market trend for the car you are interested in looks like over the next five years, stop what you are doing and go look it up. There are plenty of forecasting tools out there such as Double-Clutch and the CarGurus price trends guide. Without knowledge of where the market is heading, you could be potentially setting yourself up for failure. Never get emotionally attached to a vehicle if your goal is to try and flip it for a profit, but if you are committed for the long haul then go ahead and go all in, afterall that's why you bought an exotic car in the first place.

10 PURCHASING YOUR FIRST EXOTIC CAR

EXOTIC CAR ECONOMICS

Actual Cash Value is the lowest value that a car will fall to based on age, mileage and condition. The actual cash value is what an exotic car is worth at any given time on the open market; it's the price that you could easily sell the car for with minimal effort or resistance from a majority of buyers, including car dealers. Things that people want are always in demand and attract interest, whereas things that are tolerated out of necessity rarely produce a significant profit; therefore it is beneficial to leverage things that people actually desire and want to generate an interest in the goods, products or services that you are offering. What is the most that someone is willing to pay for something that they want? People will always find a way to "afford" the things that they want, even at the expense of certain necessities. The price you paid to purchase minus the actual cash value equals your risk exposure. You have to find a way to increase the perceived value and sell the car for more than you paid or otherwise eat the losses when you trade it in.

By learning how to play the margins, you can purchase close to or below wholesale value, and then sell within the retail margin band in order to break even or profit. Most typical retail dealerships will follow a 30 day, 60 day, 90 day rule in order to gradually step-down and reduce their listed prices, however in the case of most exotic cars (especially those on consignment) these time intervals do not apply. An exotic car can sit for years before changing owners and during that time may actually increase in value. One way to determine demand is to study and understand the Carfax report: the longer a vehicle has been in inventory, the more eager a dealer may be to sell it and move on. After 90 days most vehicles will go to the auction to be liquidated, but keep in mind again that most of the best stock of high quality exotic cars is not traded at the auctions. Remember: your money is made when you buy the car; you only collect a profit when you get ready to sell, so purchase wisely. The amount of profit (or loss) is pre-determined by how much you paid to acquire the car. As humans, we tend to overvalue what we have, and make irrational decisions about ownership. The idea of ownership makes us perceive the value of an object to be much higher if we own the object. This illustrates the phenomenon of the endowment effect which is placing a higher value on property once possession has been gained.

11 FINANCIAL STUFF TO KNOW

Get your financing straight before even attempting to negotiate a purchase. Banks don't care about your credit score to determine your loan limits; the only thing that credit score decides is how much the interest rate that the bank is going to charge, not for loan approval. Minimum credit score needs to be a 640 or better (for decent interest rate); credit basis for a car loan (only looks at payment history) pay on time and get higher approval rate. What do banks look for? Debt to income ratio, residency, employment history, loan history, credit history (banks like to see trade lines active for at least 5 years). The bank doesn't make a profit on the loan for at least 12 months after it is funded; dealer reserve, etc, after 12 months, the loan begins to generate a profit.

WHY LEASING A NEW EXOTIC CAR MAKES SENSE

To many people, one of the benchmarks of financial success involves being able to drive a high-dollar exotic car or luxury vehicle such as an Aston Martin, Bugatti, Pagani, Lamborghini, McLaren, Ferrari or hyper-luxury offering from Bentley or Rolls-Royce. To the exotic car enthusiast the prestige and pride of ownership, is worth the price of admission to experience the thrills an exotic car provides.

When the time comes to acquire a new exotic car, one of the most frequently asked questions is "how do people afford it?" The answer may come as a surprise, as many people are under the impression that exotic cars are either paid for entirely in cash (some are) or that there is some complicated lending scenario that is just as exotic as the car itself. The fact of the matter is that conventional bank loans and leasing are typically the standard, with leasing being the preferred method, and here's why:

Lease payments are typically lower. Comparing apples-to-apples, income, creditworthiness and ability to be well-qualified for approval are the same whether leasing or purchasing, however in most cases leasing a new exotic car provides fewer barriers to entry as the down payment, and subsequent monthly payments on an exotic car tend to be lower. Combine that with the fact that most exotic car leases factor in a service and maintenance plan and the total monthly operating cost is lower over the same period of time vs outright ownership.

Leasing schedules are designed to resist depreciation. Leasing schedules for an exotic car can accurately predict what the vehicle will be worth within the next 24-36 months after purchase. The monthly cost of leasing will always be less expensive vs the cost of ownership during the same time frame on a brand new exotic car, as the first owner of the exotic car takes the biggest hit due to depreciation.

Leasing is the perfect way to drive a brand new exotic car. New exotic car leases are very simple and then structured in a way that benefits both the dealership and the exotic car customer. The lease terms typically mirror the way that most exotic car owners drive, which is infrequently and sparingly as to not rack up the mileage, while alleviating a significant amount of the worries that come with traditional ownership, such as maintenance, upkeep and resale value.

Leasing a new exotic car avoids sales tax. When it comes to the "opportunity cost" associated with spending money, leasing an exotic car avoids the dreaded lump-sum sales tax that is collected when purchasing an exotic vehicle outright. Also there are tax benefits to those who are savvy enough to take advantage of the benefits that leasing and exotic car provides To those is the know, leasing has always been a lucrative financial alternative to traditional ownership, largely because it provides one of the most fiscally prudent paths to new exotic car ownership.

12 EXOTIC CARS AND SOCIAL MEDIA

LIFESTYLE AND SOCIAL INTERACTIONS

I saw a post on social media recently where a pedestrian attacked an Audi R8 owner for mildly revving his car in traffic. Also there was a video that went viral of the guy who decided to run back and forth over the top of a parked Aventador, until the owner of said car eventually had enough and threw the vandal to the ground. These real life examples are just a handful of incidents and situations that happen all the time to exotic cars and exotic car owners. So what can you do? In my experience, it's best to just stay humble, be polite and gracious. In a very literal sense, you may be the only person that a majority of people will ever meet that drives an exotic car. For many people it's like seeing an alien spaceship land; people are naturally curious about the individual that hops out of this mythological machine.

With the rise of social media sites such as Facebook, Twitter, Instagram and Snapchat, every public outing has the potential to devolve into a paparazzi-like feeding frenzy of people pointing cell phones at you and your exotic car and snapping away. People will often risk a physical beating, in order to take a picture sitting on, or standing near an exotic car, so be careful out there, because people can be unpredictable.

On an upbeat note, owning an exotic car has the potential to be used to attract positive attention and raise awareness for causes and charities that you feel passionate about. Over the years I have participated in a variety of charity car shows, rallies, and events to help promote and raise funds for everything from homeless military veterans to children with terminal illnesses. This is one of my main reasons for owning and exotic car, because I can contribute to charities that I am passionate about, and share my interest in exotic vehicles, in a way that makes me feel fulfilled and gratified. Exotic car shows are not only profitable, but also a popular way to entertain patrons of the car culture. Exotic cars, like Audis, Ferraris, Lamborghinis and Porsches, are a perineal draw and always attract a crowd at car shows and events, with eager fans clamouring to see their poster icons in real-life.

Exotic cars can be a symbol of hope and a source of inspiration to people around you. Being an influencer takes a lot of hard work and dedication. If you are really looking to develop a successful, attention grabbing social media following, then the benefits of an Exotic Car may be just what you need. Anything that you can use as a hook to grow your audience and help you stand out from the crowd is a good thing, so be creative in your usage of exotic cars and the exotic car culture.

13 WAYS TO PROFIT FROM EXOTIC CARS

THERE ARE 3 BILLION SOCIAL MEDIA USERS ONLINE.
Exotic cars are a highly visible platform that garner lots of attention and so they are a great way to get people's attention and raise people's awareness to your brand or cause. It's never been easier to start making money from the internet. Thanks to the power of the internet, you can create direct-to-consumer relationships that will allow you to curate an audience who knows and loves your brand, and directly supports your business.

WHO'S REAPING THE PROFIT?
If you've ever shared a picture, video, comment, blog post or article on the internet congratulations: you are a content creator! The big question is how are you leveraging your contributions to your advantage and what are you receiving from your work? And it is work. Consider this for a moment: actors, authors, artists, comedians, composers, critics, celebrities, journalists, photographers, poets, designers, directors, entertainers writers and the list goes on and on. What do these people all have in common? They are all occupations that have the potential to receive compensation and generate income from their work. What's the difference between them and you? Nothing but a label and a little intentional effort. Actions that you take every day whether conscious or otherwise send a message to the people around you that you interact with and influence. You influence people with how you

dress and wear (you're a fashion model), you give your opinion and review products (you're a professional critic), you post pictures and videos (you're a photographer) you are a prolific writer and like to blog (you're an author) there are many more examples that I can cited, but you get the general idea. With a little focus and some deliberate effort you can transform your hobby or casual interests into something that can offset your every day expenses and in many cases generate a positive net profit. And why shouldn't you? There are businesses all around you that are benefiting from you every single day.

BUILD YOUR OWN BRAND

You can make significant income from leveraging exotic cars on social media. If you want attention on social media, all you need to do is share a picture of your exotic car. There's actually a way to make a profit from exotic cars, even if you don't own them. What's more, there are many avenues that will enable you to drive exotic cars to generate profits. Advertising on social media platforms like YouTube, Facebook and Instagram are the most obvious, accessible way is to capitalize on being an exotic car enthusiast. Building your social network, becoming an influencer, providing outlets for mainstream advertising or using affiliate marketing is are simple ways to generate passive income as an exotic car social media entrepreneur.

CONTROL YOUR CONTENT

By leveraging your following to provide direct marketing solutions and charging a fee for 'post mentions' and shout-outs, you can easily justify the cost and expense of having your own exotic car. Large social followings on Facebook, YouTube, Instagram and Snapchat appeal to advertisers trying to reach the niche or target demographic that you have cultivated. The target audience for the exotic car segment is typically dominated by males between the ages of 16 and 35, allowing advertisers to laser focus their offers to appeal to consumers in that range.

MONETIZE YOUR ONLINE ACTIVITIES

Most people haven't got a clue about how to properly utilize an Exotic Car to boost and increase their business. While it may sound incredulous to buy a new exotic car solely for business purposes, there are actually many key benefits to investing in one of these vehicles, as long as it's the "right" vehicle. With the proper business structure, an exotic car can be leveraged as a great advertising platform, lead generator and brand builder. Exotic cars attract a lot of attention, which in turn can help stimulate interest and create new customers. In most cases, with proper planning, your exotic car will pay for itself.

SEVERAL WAYS TO MAKE MONEY WITH EXOTIC CARS

1. Do you own an exotic car? Use it to advertise your business and drive for free.

2. Do you like taking photos? Sell images, prints and graphics of exotic cars, or better yet take professional pictures and charge a fee.

3. Do you have a large social media following or influence? Become a social media marketer, and sell paid advertising to help brands grow.

4. Are you a talented writer, blogger, or vlogger? Create a website or YouTube channel and sell items, or even your own merchandise.

5. Arbitrage. Find and buy exotic cars and resell them for a profit or even better.

6. Become an auto broker and find and negotiate deals for your clients and customers and charge them a fee.

7. Start a Luxury car rental company and rent out your car on sites like Turo or Uber Black.

8. Start a business that caters to exotic car owners, like concierge, mobile detailing, or a valet service.

9. Open an exotic car customization shop

10. Get your dealer's license and open your own exotic car dealership.

PROTECT YOUR INTELLECTUAL PROPERTY

Incorporate, Copyright, Trademark, Watermark. Everything from the clothes you wear, the type of car you drive and what/where you eat and drink are sources of free advertising and marketing for the respective brand owners. You might get the pride of ownership, but the brands reap the profits. The message that you are sending as an unintentional brand ambassador is that you endorse the products that you use and the brands that you are wearing. Celebrities and professional models get paid millions of dollars to advertise a brand. And companies spend billions of dollars on advertising and marketing in order to reach their target audience. In essence your are paying to advertise someone else's business. Wouldn't it be nice to control the message, or at least get something for your efforts instead of a warm fuzzy feeling and an empty wallet? Now you can and it's never been easier to create and control your own brand by managing and leveraging your content contributions. You have the power of creative control.

14 GETTING PAID TO DRIVE EXOTIC CARS

YOU, INCORPORATED

So the very first thing that you need to do is start a business. Owning your own business (any business for that matter) is the single most important and valuable endeavor you can undertake in order to achieve financial success and improve your life **TODAY**. I personally recommend that you form a business entity and incorporate.

Formal incorporation into something like an LLC or S-corp with a unique EIN helps to legitimize your endeavors and lend credibility to your efforts. Also, the tax advantages of owning your own business are numerous and very beneficial. Everyday things that you are probably doing right now take on a different context when performed in the course of normal business operations. Social media platforms capitalize on your efforts and profit from your willingness to participate and interact with others using their platform. Imagine the hours of entertainment and free content that is being created by users across various social media sites such as facebook, Instagram, Twitter and YouTube. When a tweet or video goes viral, in most cases the person who is the focus or subject of the story goes completely uncredited and receives no monetary compensation, even though their actions and images are being widely used and published across the internet.

A NOTE ABOUT MONTANA LLCS

I'm sure that by now you have heard about or seen exotic cars driving around on out-of-state plates from places such as Montana. The reason being that there are definite tax advantages to having an expensive exotic car registered in the state of Montana. I won't go into much detail regarding the nuances and pros vs cons of doing a Montana or similar registration except to say that it can be a legitimate way to mitigate tax exposure when purchasing an exotic vehicle for business purposes. Check with your tax advisor or legal professional regarding your individual situation, however it can be a very effective way to leverage incorporating a business in a tax friendly environment in order to minimize your tax liability when purchasing an exotic car for profit.

FOCUS ON YOUR NICHE

Decide what aspect of the business you want to be involved with and then focus on ways to provide value within that segment of the market. For example, I own an Exotic Car Brokering and Consignment company. I decided to only focus on providing services to clients seeking to purchase or sell luxury and exotic vehicles. By working with a very small, and select group of clientele, I am able to offer a very high level of service at a competitive price. Lower volume typically equates to higher profit margins, as you are providing a higher quality product to a limited audience. So think about who your ideal customer is and focus on going above and beyond what anyone else in your niche or segment is doing. Under promise, but always over deliver.

THINK OUTSIDE THE BOX: DISRUPTIVE INNOVATION

Regardless of what you decide to pursue as your focus, make sure that you are able to creatively include an exotic car as an essential element in your business.

If you are a mobile detailer for example, make sure that you use your exotic car as a display vehicle to showcase the quality of your work. The same thing applies to anyone doing vehicle customization and repairs such as vehicle tuning shops, aftermarket modifications, vinyl wraps and graphics or even racing. If you have a business or organization that you are involved in, an exotic car can make a very effective rolling advertisement in order to generate interest and create leads for your business. Also, exotic car rental as a business has become more accessible that ever thanks to companies like Turo, Uber, Lyft etc and their various ride-sharing platforms. At the end of the day, being able to find creative ways to utilize your exotic car in your own personal business is the most effective way of converting a depreciating liability into a valuable asset.

FINAL THOUGHTS AND OBSERVATIONS

Exotic cars can either be a very costly sign of wealth and status, or alternately they can be a source of income and profit. According to signaling theory, it is believed that owning an exotic car produces benefits in social interactions, eliciting responses such as preferential treatment and in some cases even financial benefits aka Status-dependent favorable treatment.

Whether all of this is true or not, I don't really know. I can't say for sure if owning an exotic car in and of itself will open any doors for you (although I have had quite a few doors opened for me since buying an exotic car) but I will say that it has increased my awareness as to how other people perceive objects of affluence, and also presented me with additional opportunities for interactions that I did not previously know existed. For example, many years ago I wanted to buy a used Mitsubishi 3000 and was turned away by a salesman at the local franchise dealership because he said that I looked too young and he doubted that I could afford the car. At the time I had already purchased and paid off a brand new Eagle Talon Tsi (which was as expensive as the Mitsubishi if not more) had a perfect credit score, a co-signer and $10,000 cash burning a hole in my pocket. I received a call later that day from the owner of the dealership, who issued a profuse apology and invitation to come back and buy the car, but too little too late, I'd already moved on and purchased a new Nissan 300Z. Fast forward to today where

I've owned and driven several Porsches, Audi R8s, Ferraris, Aston Martins, Lamborghinis, Bentleys and more, and I can walk into most highline dealerships and routinely test drive the most expensive exotic cars that they have. How the times have changed!

In closing, I hope that that you found this brief guide helpful, and useful in your own pursuit of your first exotic car. In my experience, I can say that at some point and time, most people will encounter these scenarios to various degrees, but hopefully the positive experiences and the good times will outweigh any negative aspects of owning an exotic car. The complete depth and breadth of the world of exotic cars is such that it cannot be easily summed up in a few pages. By using broad strokes, hopefully I have shared some tidbits of knowledge and the high points of my own exotic car buying experiences and how I have profited from them, both financially and socially. Feel free to contact me with any specific questions to keep the conversation going, I would love to hear about your exotic car ownership experiences.

Sincerely,

Dee Oneal

ABOUT THE AUTHOR

Growing up I was always surrounded by cars. Not just exotic cars, but automobiles in general. My dad was a heavy equipment mechanic and my mom was a serial entrepreneur-business owner, so coming from that background I sought out opportunities to merge the two worlds. I spent countless hours working on cars with my dad, helping with everything from oil changes to complete engine rebuilds. One of my first jobs was working in my uncle's auto body repair shop learning how to paint and restore cars. I also had an uncle who owned a major franchise dealership, which would come in handy in the years to come.

When I went off to college, I worked as a detailer at the local car wash in order to supplement my income. It wasn't until I worked as a valet that I acquired a taste for exotic cars. Even then they weren't nearly as interesting to me as the popular import car culture that was rapidly gaining attention. One of my first independent business ventures was to capitalize on the booming import car craze, and I opened my very own import tuning shop. Things we're great up until the time when the economy took a dive around 2008 and the market contracted and the economy took a nosedive. During the lean years I worked diligently to refine my skills in the automobile industry doing everything from car rentals, car sales, consulting and remarketing.

It was around 2013 that the opportunity came for me to once again apply the knowledge I had gained from my many years in the automobile industry to capitalize on the emerging luxury and exotic car market, and as they say the rest is history. As the owner of several Porsches and my personal favorite exotic car, the Audi R8, I can say with utmost certainty that now is the best time to be alive for any exotic car enthusiast. The rise of social media and internet marketing has made it easier than ever before for anyone to build a business that can reach your target audience and rival the biggest and best brands in the world. The power truly belongs to the people.

Visit us on the web at:
www.exoticcarfacts.com

© 2018 Exotic Car Facts